THE AR

SUN TZU

ADAPTED FOR THE CONTEMPORARY
READER BY JAMES HARRIS

ISBN: 9798634927077

TABLE OF CONTENTS

INTRODUCTION 5

CHAPTER 1 - LAYING PLANS 6

CHAPTER 2 - WAGING WAR 15

CHAPTER 3 - ATTACK BY STRATAGEM 20

CHAPTER 4 - TACTICAL DISPOSITIONS 26

CHAPTER 5 - ENERGY 31

CHAPTER 6 - WEAK AND STRONG POINTS.....................37

CHAPTER 7 - MANAUVERING 45

CHAPTER 8 - VARIATION OF TACTICS 54

CHAPTER 9 -AN ARMY ON THE MARCH.........................61

CHAPTER 10 - TERRAIN 71

CHAPTER 11 - THE NINE SITUATIONS 80

CHAPTER 12 - THE ATTACK BY FIRE 98

CHAPTER 13 - THE USE OF SPIES 104

INTRODUCTION

I'm sure you have heard about 'The Art of War', which has led you to this book. Perhaps you have read it before and did not quite understand it all, or this may be your first time attempting to comprehend this marvellous work. The work in itself already has been revered for centuries, however, times change, nothing can be left without upkeep forever, that only leads to degeneration and ruin. I will not let this book be forgotten and have renewed it for our current times, to help keep this book relevant for more centuries to come with my name attached to it – until sometime in the year 3000, it will again need an update – of course by that time the war will be in cyber/space, the war between your brain and technology, a war between man and man-made creation. You may already see it emerging. Regardless of what's to come, there are wars to fight right now. WAR is not reserved for countries, we have our own individual wars within our very lives. Are you ready to declare war on all that troubles you? Unceasing war. Relentless war. If war is needed, war is coming. If war is what they want, war is what they will get.

CHAPTER 1 - LAYING PLANS

1. Sun Tzu said: The art of war is of vital importance to the State.

No doubt you are reading this, and you are not 'the State', yet – the work contained herein can be applied to any ruling body. As in you, you are a 'body', and you may rule. Rule your life and your realm.

2. It is a matter of life and death, a road either to safety or to ruin. Hence it is a subject of inquiry which can on no account be neglected.

If you want to rule, to lead yourself and/or others, along with your life in the direction you want to go, you cannot overlook 'The Art of War'. There is no need to attach a negative connotation to the word 'War' it is of utmost importance, because unfortunately within our reality there are those that want to see your downfall, and may even work toward it, and additionally the general nature of life leads us on the path to inevitable destruction which is inescapable, but we must fight, fight to delay the end (look after ourselves), and fight to overcome the challenges of life – whilst simultaneously enjoying it to the fullest.

3. The art of war, then, is governed by five constant factors, to be considered in one's deliberations, when seeking to determine the conditions of the field.

What is the field? Wars are not always fought on a field, as in a green space of land, but the term 'field' can be applied to any endeavour, arena or market place (for those in business), which is entered in to for the purpose of war/winning.

4. These are:

1. The Moral Law.
2. Heaven.
3. Earth.
4. The Commander.
5. Method and discipline.

5 & 6. The Moral Law causes the people to be in complete accord with their ruler, so that they will follow him regardless of their lives, undismayed by any danger.

As rulers of ourselves, we must be in alignment with our own moral laws, so that we may be in complete accord with our ruler, ie: ourselves. By doing so, we may follow ourselves, our judgement, gut feelings, and true-life paths without fear and in perfect harmony with our inner feelings.

Tu Yu quotes Wang Tzu as saying: "Without constant practice, the officers will be nervous and indecisive when assembling for battle; without constant practice, the general will be uncertain and irresolute when the crisis is at hand."

War requires constant attention, daily focus, and never-ending discipline in preparation. It cannot be half-hearted, haphazard, hear and there, now and then, it is a daily duty to be preparing for war – so that when the time comes, you will be fearless, and you are as ready as you can be for the day of battle. Get started now, there is no time to waste. Do not wait for the battle to come without preparing for it today. This applies to anything you wish to undertake/achieve, without consistent preparation, drilling the basics to reinforce them, and then building upon them consistently day in day out, when the day comes, you will be underprepared, uncertain, lack confidence and all of this will be easily noticed by the enemy. The term 'Enemy' does not have to be used to signify a person, it could be used as a term for any upcoming challenges which occur during any pursuit.

7. Heaven signifies night and day, cold and heat, times and seasons.

The seeds are planted in spring for the harvest in autumn. We are not just talking about the weather here and when it is best to be on a battlefield, this metaphor applies beyond the elements, to seasonal changes in business environments, the trends (current and forthcoming), the best times to sow and the best times to reap, the time to start, the time to stop, the time to exert energy, the time to rest – all must be calibrated and suited to that which is being undertaken..

8. Earth comprises distances, great and small; danger and security; open ground and narrow passes; the chances of life and death.

The landscape, the terrain, the market, the environment you are in, or wish to enter – needs to be assessed to the best of your ability. Not all will be visible initially, but one must take the time to observe and take note of all which can be seen/researched now – but make this also something which is constantly reassessed and expanded upon – as all domains (and life for the matter), are never fixed, and are always in a state of perpetual change.

9. The Commander stands for the virtues of:

1. Wisdom.
2. Sincerity.
3. Benevolence.
4. Courage.
5. Strictness.

The five cardinal virtues of the Chinese are:

1. Humanity or benevolence.
2. Uprightness of mind.
3. Self-respect & self-control.
4. Wisdom.
5. Sincerity or good faith.

The traditional Chinese virtues substitute uprightness of mind for courage, and self-respect/self-control for strictness.

It's interesting to note that the order is different for the two sets of virtues yet comprise the same. It may be taken that these virtues require to be prioritised in a different order from time to time, but the commander, or anyone undertaking war should not be without any of them.

10. Method and discipline means the organising of the army in its proper subdivisions, the graduations of rank among the officers, the maintenance of roads by which supplies may reach the army, and control of military expenditure.

Subdivisions and graduations of rank are of importance in any endeavour, subdivisions let one know the current position, and rank graduations act as road maps to development and clear milestones toward the height of achievement.

Maintain all roads which transport supplies to the army and the ruler, IE: you. This can be interpreted as income, food, resources, relationships etc. and the subsequent control in terms of using these resources is something to be considered and managed well.

11. The five constant factors listed in point (4) – and explained in points 5-10, should be familiar to every general: he who knows them will be victorious; he does not will fail.

12. In your deliberations, when seeking to determine the military conditions, let them be made on the basis of a comparison, in the following manner:

13.

1. Which of the two generals, are the followers most loyal to?
2. Which of the two generals understand the seasons best?
3. Who has assessed the earth and understands the terrain better than the other?
4. Which commander possesses the five virtues in greater strength?
5. Which army is stronger, morally as well as physically?
6. On which side is discipline most rigorously enforced?

7. On which side are officers and men more highly trained?
8. In which army is there the greater consistency in both reward and punishment?
9. On which side is there the most absolute certainty that merit will be properly rewarded and misdeeds appropriately punished?

14. By means of these considerations I can forecast victory or defeat.

15. The general that listens to my advice and acts upon it, will conquer, and remain in command! The general that does not listen to my advice or act upon it, will suffer defeat, and will be dismissed!

16. While benefiting from the profit of my advice, you may also gain from any helpful circumstances over and above the ordinary rules.

This advice does not only give one guaranteed victory, beyond victory, comes greater rewards for the conqueror.

17. When circumstances are favourable, one should modify plans accordingly.

Don't now allow favourable times and seasons to give you comfort. Plans must always, be continuously laid, and thought out in advance of what is to come.

18. All warfare is based on deception.

19. Hence, when able to attack, we must seem unable; when using our forces, we must seem inactive; when we are near, we must make the enemy believe we are far away; when far away, we must make him believe we are near.

The general must be discreet, all plans must be kept closely guarded, but commenced in sequence according to prepared action points. Without the enemy knowing what is to come next. Whatever the general is doing, he must appear to not be doing.

20. Entice the enemy with bait. For example: appear disordered, to lure the enemy and then crush him.

Appear weak when fully prepared, strong and ready to destroy. By appearing weak, if the enemy advances, it is really the enemy that is potentially weak as he has been tricked in to a false sense of confidence.

21. If he is secure at all points, be prepared for him. If he is in superior strength, evade him.

If the general senses that the enemy is strong, then he must be fully prepared for battle, but if the enemy is of superior strength the general must evade attack, although this only indicates that the general was not ready to lure the enemy to advance.

22. If the enemy is easily angered, irritate him.

A good tactician plays with the enemy like a cat plays with a mouse. At one moment laying still, appearing lifeless, and the next, pouncing on him.

23. If he is taking his ease, give him no rest. If his forces are united, separate them.

Do not let the enemy rest, when it is clear he needs rest, provoke him. On the other hand, when you require rest, tire him out by luring him in the wrong direction.

24. Attack him where he is unprepared, appear where you are not expected.

The enemy should never expect your presence – and should not even have an indication of your potential appearance.

25. All military strategies which lead to victory, should not be made known beforehand.

Never reveal any plans before action, it is too risky, enemies may intercept the plans and pin-point areas of weakness and thwart them before they even begin.

26. The general who makes many calculations in his office before the war is fought, will be victorious.

Every general must have a place from which to devise plans and calculate movements. A specific place carved out for this purpose only. In business, this is generally an office space.

A general who makes very little calculations loses the battle before it starts.

The result of insufficient planning is always failure. Fail to plan > plan to fail.

Therefore, many calculations and recalculations are required for the general to be victorious, and few calculations lead to failure. Based on who has calculated the most, it becomes apparent who is likely to win or lose.

CHAPTER 2 - WAGING WAR

For those who wish to fight, first they must count the cost.

1. Sun Tzu said: In war one must estimate costs for transportation and soldiers, the expenditure must be accounted for, at home and away, including the cost of small items such as glue to the largest of sums spent on vehicles and armour.

What is the cost of the war you wish to wage? This must be determined to understand if the war is worth it. What will be gained from this war? If the potential return outweighs the cost – the war may be considered worthwhile, but keep in mind that perhaps there are better wars to wage, which require less expenditure for an even greater return.

2. When engaging in combat, if the length of time taken for victory is great, then men's weapons will wear out, and their enthusiasm will weaken.

Take in to consideration the expenditure of time for the reward of victory. That which takes longer to achieve requires great patience and a thorough understanding of the energy required to maintain momentum and enthusiasm. If this is not given consideration beforehand, and fully understood, one may find themselves growing impatient and tired from prolonged and persistent effort.

3. If the time in war extends beyond what was expected, the resources of the State will also be depleted further.

Wars that continue beyond the length of time expected continue to drain funds, resources and energy. The potential for extensions must always be included in the pre-calculations, and contingencies set aside.

4. When your weapons are worn out, your enthusiasm weakened, your strength diminished and your funds exhausted, other generals will seek to take advantage of your position. Then no man, however wise he may be, will be able to prevent the consequences that follow.

You never want to find yourself in this position. Carefully consider wars which lead to this state – and avoid them if possible. Long protracted wars are the most energy intense, resource and fund consuming.

5. Therefore, although we have heard numerous times that only fools rush in, its opposite: intelligence, is not as commonly associated with long delays.

Delay war where necessary, especially if it leads to certain depletion of resources and energy without significant gain. Only wars with definitive victory and reward are worthwhile.

It has been said that rushing in is stupid, however one may win through sheer force and speed. Haste may actually save energy and funds. Protracted operations can be clever but come with heavy expenditure. The difficulty of lengthy operations entails: an aging army, expenditure of wealth, an empty exchequer and distress for the ordinary citizens; true genius ensures against such disaster.

As long as victory can be achieved, haste is much more preferable than clever protracted operations. However, in some cases it is preferable to not begin a war at all, if not true gain is to be made.

6. No country has ever benefited from prolonged warfare.

7. Only one who fully understands the real costs of war can calculate profitable ways of carrying it out.

As is the case with all things, if the costs are not understood, along with what is to be attained for the expenditure, profit cannot be calculated at all.

8. A skilful soldier does not raise secondary funding for the same project, and his supplies will not need replenishing.

Once war is declared, the skilful soldier will not waste precious time waiting for reinforcements, and will not turn his army around for further supplies, instead he crosses the enemy's border without delay. This may seem like a very risky strategy to recommend, but all great strategists, from Julius Caesar to Napoleon Bonaparte, have mentioned how valued timeliness is, as being ahead of your opponent has counted for more than numerical superiority or the greatest calculations in regard to supplies and equipment.

9. Bring the materials necessary from home, but take from the enemy. Therefore, the army will always have enough required for its needs.

10. Depletion of funds requires an army to be maintained by contributions from the treasury. Further contributions to maintain an army from a distance causes the citizens to be impoverished.

11. On the other hand, close proximity of an army causes price rises; and higher prices cause the people's wealth to be drained away.

In any case the cost of war cannot be avoided, from a distance an army requires indirect funds from the citizens in the form of taxes which are distributed, and when close by the army may take what is required directly from the citizens, for example food from the fields, which consequently drive prices up, which bring about another indirect cost of war.

12. When the citizen's wealth has been drained away, the heavily afflicted will grow angry and demand compensation.

13, 14. With the loss of wealth and strength, the homes of the citizens will become bare, and a large portion of their income will be dissipated.

15. Therefore a wise general deliberately takes what they can from the enemy. One load of the enemy's provisions is worth more than one's own.

It requires effort and energy to transport supplies, if these can be taken from the enemy, one saves themself the expenditure required to transport provisions.

16. To kill the enemy, the army must be angered, and fully buy in to the idea that there will be advantage in defeating the enemy, and their reward for doing so will be secured.

All must be able to see the reward of their effort, from the top to the very bottom. Those who lead the war will have specific advantages to be gained, and those who form the base, the soldiers must have adequate rewards to look forward to. Anything that is captured from the enemy must be used as either a resource or converted in to a reward for all, which gives every man a strong desire to fight and reap the rewards of his effort.

17. Therefore in chariot fighting, when ten or more chariots have been taken, those should be rewarded who took the first. Our own flags should be substituted for those of the enemy, and the chariots mingled and used in conjunction with ours. The captured soldiers should be kindly treated and kept.

18. By doing so the conquered soldiers are used to amplify one's own strength.

19. Therefore, in war, let your greatest objective be victory, not lengthy campaigns.

War is not something to be frightened by – which is the main lesson Sun Tzu intends to convey in this chapter.

20. It must be known that the people's fate rests upon the shoulders of the army's general, a man who has the power to determine whether the nation will be peace or in danger.

CHAPTER 3 - ATTACK BY STRATAGEM

1. Sun Tzu said: In the practical art of war, the best thing of all is to take the enemy's country whole and intact; to shatter and destroy it is not a good idea. Likewise, it is better to capture an army entirely than to destroy it totally.

Why destroy what you can keep? By doing so, it then becomes useless to both you and the enemy. Where is the reward in total destruction? Only destroy what is necessary, with a view to capture as much as possible in a useable condition.

2. Therefore, to fight and conquer in all your battles is not supreme excellence; supreme excellence consists in breaking through your enemy's resistance without fighting.

3. The highest form of strategy is to ruin the enemy's plans.

Sun Tzu believed that in war, it is to be considered that the enemy is plotting against us, as we are against them. But before the war evolves, the highest form of strategy is to foil their plans. As explained earlier war always leads to depletion – therefore less energy can be expended by strategizing how to ruin the enemies plans.

4. Never attempt to attack a walled city if it can be avoided.

If ruining the enemy's plans is not achieved, the next best strategy is to battle in the field, but as mentioned above, at all costs – one should avoid trying to attack a walled city. It is the worst strategy of all. The enemy is heavily defenced and the exertion to break through will lead to a substantial loss of power.

The transportation of shields, relocatable barracks, and essential equipment may take months. Therefore:

5. The general who is unable to control his emotions, will send his men to attack like swarming ants.

Slow progress in war may provoke impatience in a general who is unable to control the emotions. This lack of patience and irrationality will cause him to not heed the warning above 'never attack a walled city'. It will lead to the destruction of his soldiers and the city will still not be taken. This is the disastrous effect of an irrational siege.

6. Therefore, a skilful general will pacify the enemy's soldiers without fighting; he conquers their cities without besieging them, and takes over their kingdom without protracted operations. But, he only dismantles the government and does not harm the people.

7. By keeping his army intact he will reveal the flaws in the current Empire, and without losing a single man, his victory will be complete. With his weapons still sharp, their zeal remains. This is to attack by stratagem.

8. The rule of war is as follows: if we outnumber the enemy 10 to 1 we surround him; if five to one, we attack him

(without the need for any further advantage), if we have double the enemy's soldiers we divide our army in two.

This is straight forward, 10 – 1 allows to surround the enemy from all sides, 5 – 1 allows for a strong attack, and double the enemy's soldiers allows to split the army in two (misleading the enemy in to a head on attack with one half, while the other half closes in from behind.

9. When we are equally matched we can always offer a fight.

If the soldiers are equal in number, then it is only the generals that fight. In some cases, the number of soldiers may differ to some degree, but this can be made up with superior strength or better discipline. Equal in this case means an evenly balanced match whether the numbers are equal or not. If outnumbered avoid the enemy.

10. A relentless fight may be initiated by a small force, but in the end, it must be ended by a larger force.

Any fight – ends through excess of power, and where one side must yield to the other. Two equally matched opponents will maintain a protracted war, until one or the other weakens, and one retains strength sufficient enough to win.

11. If the general's walls surrounding the State are fortified at all points; the State will be strong; if the walls are defective, the State will be weak.

Strong defence is a key element in the art of war, for the general's own safety and that of those under the protection of the general. All that has been attained and acquired must be protected, Strong defence must be put in to place to not only protect against threats, but to deter them. The general must be well educated in his profession.

12. There are three ways that a general can cause damage to his own army:

13. (1) By commanding his army to move forward or to retreat, being ignorant of the fact that they cannot do so. This is called hobbling the army.

It would appear that if a general is commanding his army to do something they cannot do that he must be far removed from the field. While a general should not be in the thick of the war, and should be slightly removed from the field, his distance should not be so far that he cannot see what is happening. If this occurs – he is unable to view the position and will make errors in his calculations, thus leading to irrelevant orders.

In summary: a general must take an overview of the battle, but not be completely detached.

14. (2) By attempting to control an army in the same way as he manages the kingdom. This causes unrest in the soldiers' minds.

Civilian life is a completely different arena to that of the military. The military requires opportunism and flexibility –

whereas the general population requires more rigidity. Trying to impose too much structure on a soldier will eventually lead to unrest. Although structure is necessary, the soldier also requires the ability to be flexible and adapt, to think on his feet and this allows for quick decisions and rapid movement where necessary. People who operate like this in general society are usually out of the box characters, such as entrepreneurs.

15. (3) Being indiscriminate when selecting his officers, especially by placing those who are unable to adapt. This does damage to the confidence of the soldiers that serve under him.

If a general has no understanding of adaptability, he cannot be trusted with a position of authority. The skilful general looks for four types of people and places them in their appropriate positions:

1. *A wise man*
2. *A brave man*
3. *A desirous man*
4. *A foolish man*

The wise man delights in displaying his wisdom.
The brave man displays his courage in battle.
The desirous man seeks and profits from opportunities.
And the foolish man does not fear death.

16. When the army is distrustful of the leader, difficulties are sure to arise from the enemy. This brings disorder in to the army, and throws victory away.

17. Therefore we must know the five essentials for victory:

(1) Clearly knowing when to fight and when not to fight.

If he is able to fight, he attacks, if he is unable to attack he withdraws. He who knows when to attack and when to withdraw will win.

(2) Knowing how to handle both superior and inferior forces.

This is not purely knowing how to estimate the size and power of the enemy's army, but applying the art of war to defeat an army of any size. Attention must be paid to the location, and timing. If the general leads a superior force he must make the ground easy for the enemy, thus luring them to him; if he meets with a superior army he must make the ground difficult encouraging them not to attack.

(3) Animating the army with the same spirit throughout all its ranks.

(4) Being fully prepared, and waiting to take the enemy unprepared.

(5) Having full military capacity and no interference from the sovereign.

The sovereign may give broad instructions, but should in no way interfere thereafter with battles and wars, the strategy and leadership of the army is for the general alone.

18. If you know yourself and the enemy, you will not fear the result of a hundred battles. If you know yourself but not

the enemy, for every victory gained you will also suffer a defeat.

Knowing the enemy enables you to attack, knowing yourself enables you to defend. Attack is the secret of defence; defence is the planning of an attack.

CHAPTER 4 - TACTICAL DISPOSITIONS

Through the dispositions of an army its condition may be discovered. Conceal your dispositions, and your condition remains a secret, which leads to victory; show your dispositions, and your condition will become recognizable, which leads to defeat. A good general secures success by modifying his tactical dispositions to meet those of the enemy.

1. Good fighters place themselves beyond any possibility of defeat, and wait for an opportunity to defeat the enemy.

2. The power to secure ourselves against defeat is within our own hands, but the opportunity to defeat the enemy is provided by the enemy, due to a mistake on his part.

3. Therefore a good fighter can secure himself against defeat, by concealing the disposition of his soldiers, covering his tracks, and taking constant precautions, however this does not guarantee defeating the enemy.

4. Which leads to the saying: one may know how to win without being able to do it.

5. Security against defeat implies defensive tactics; ability to defeat the enemy means taking the offensive.

Defence is of importance to secure against defeat, however, he who only takes the defensive can never win.

6. Being purely defensive indicates insufficient strength; attacking, indicates and abundance of strength.

7. The general who is skilled in defence hides in the recesses of the earth.

Hiding in the recesses of the earth is a metaphor meaning that he who is in defensive mode will hide in secrecy and concealment so the enemy will not know where he is or what he is doing. A general skilled in attacking flashes from the heights of heaven – meaning he appears like a thunderbolt out of nowhere, and gives no time for the enemy to prepare. On one hand we have the ability to protect ourselves, but on the other we may secure victory.

8. To gain victory against common people is not the pinnacle of excellence.

To see the plant before it has germinated, and foresee the event before the action has begun: is excellence.

9. Neither is it the pinnacle of excellence if you fight and conquer and the whole world says, "well done!"

To plan in secret, to move covertly, to foil the enemy's intentions and ruin his plans, so any war may be won without shedding a drop of blood: is excellence.

10. To lift a hair is no sign of superior strength; to see the sun is no sign of sharp sight; to hear thunder is no sign of great hearing.

Strength, sharp sight and great hearing are all required for the superior general. One should be able to lift extremely heavy objects, see small objects at great distance, and hear the footsteps of an ant.

11. A clever fighter is not only one that wins, but excels at winning with ease.

One who can only see what is obvious, may win a battle with great difficulty; but one who can look deeply in to things, wins with ease.

12. Victories do not bring a great general reputation for his wisdom or credit for his courage.

A truly great general wins battles that the general public have no awareness of. His victories are gained over circumstances that are not known by all. Therefore, he gains no reputation for his wisdom or credit for his courage.

13. He wins his battles by making no mistakes.

A great general does not plan excessive operations or unnecessary attacks. One who seeks to win purely with sheer strength, as skilled as he may be, can be defeated; whereas one who can peek into the future and foresee events not yet manifest, will never make an error and therefore consistently win.

If no mistakes are made victory is guaranteed, because it means conquering enemies that are already defeated.

14.Therefore, a skilful fighter makes his defeat impossible, but does not miss an opportunity to defeat the enemy.

To secure against defeat a wise general will put everything in place which protects himself and his army.

15. Therefore, in war the grand strategist only seeks battle after the victory has been won, but he who is destined for defeat seeks to fight first and afterwards aims for victory.

First one must strategize victory and formulate plans with ensure victory. If you rely on strength alone victory cannot be assured.

16. The greatest general cultivates moral laws, and strictly adheres to his methods and discipline; therefore, it is always in his power to control his success.

17. The military methods are as follows:

    1. Measurement.
    2. Estimating quantities.
    3. Calculation.
    4. Balancing chance.
    5. Victory.

18.

- Measurement is derived from the terrain.
- Estimating quantities from measurement
- Calculation from estimating quantities
- Balancing chance from calculation
- Victory from balancing chance.

Measurement is the initial starting point, at which one views the terrain, the environment, the conditions, the opposing army and the challenge that lies ahead. From this one can estimate the quantity of soldiers and resources required for battle. After which, the general calculates all potential possibilities and what if scenarios. After having done so, the general weighs up his calculations to determine how strongly victory is guaranteed. The general then knows if victory is guaranteed.

19. A victorious army opposing a defeated one, is like a kilogram against gram.

A general with a history of winning vs a general with a history of losing, is essentially like a kilo of weight verses a mere gram.

20. The continual progressive momentum of a conquering force is like water ready to burst a dam.

Progressive momentum, gathers with each victory, until it can no longer be contained, and rushes forward forging its path.

CHAPTER 5 - ENERGY

1. Controlling a large force is the same as controlling a small one: it is as simple as dividing the numbers.

This simply means, to divide the army into regiments, or the corporation in to smaller companies or branches each with someone subordinate to command them.

2. Fighting with a large army under your control is no different than fighting with a small one: it only requires the introduction of signals and signs.

3. To ensure your army remains unshaken by the enemy's attacks is achieved through direct and indirect manoeuvres.

The general must be active, yet passive. Passive means to wait for the right opportunity, but ready to strike with action when it presents itself. A direct manoeuvre can be considering as one that is frontal and visible, whereas an indirect maneuverer would be to attack from the rear, surprisingly and catching the enemy off guard and unaware. Therefore, a general would always favour indirect manoeuvres as he never wants his attacks to be perceived before they occur.

4. That the impact of your army can be like a hammer against an egg, and this can be achieved by studying the weak and strong points.

5. In all warfare, direct methods are used for joining a battle, but indirect methods are required to secure victory.

Be in the habit of developing indirect tactics, so the movements of the army are not to be perceived – and the attacks come suddenly without warning.

6. Indirect tactics, when efficiently applied, are inexhaustible like the earth, and unending like the flow of rivers and streams, they end and begin again: like the four seasons, they pass and return.

7. Five musical notes, in various combinations can create more melodies than can ever be heard.

8. Five primary colours (blue, yellow, red, white, and black), in various combinations can produce more hues than can ever been seen.

9 Five tastes (sour, acidic, salted, sweet, bitter) in various combinations can produce more flavours than can ever be tasted.

10. However in battle, there are only two methods of attack: direct and indirect; yet these two in combination create an endless series of manoeuvres.

11. The direct and the indirect lead on to each other like moving in a circle, and never end. Their combination is inexhaustible.

12. The arrival of soldiers is like a strong and fast-moving stream that will even move stones along with it.

13. The quality of decision is like the well-timed dive from an eagle which enables it to strike and destroy its prey.

14. Therefore the good fighter will strike with tremendous force, but first be sure of his decision.

15. Energy: is like bending the crossbow; decision: is releasing the trigger.

16. During the disarray and commotion of war, there may be disorder, but no real disorder at all; among the confusion and chaos, your army may appear to be in bewilderment, yet it will be not be defeated.

Although the army may appear to be disordered, this is part of the various signals agreed, and part of plans that are formulated to confuse the enemy. The formation of the soldiers may appear chaotic yet there is no chaos as this is a preconceived plan and all soldiers are actively working in correct formation.

17. Simulated disorder is actually discipline, simulated fear is actually courage; simulated weakness is actually strength.

To simulate confusion to lure the enemy requires great discipline. Displaying fear to make the enemy advance leading them in to a trap takes great courage. Appearing as weak to make the enemy over-confident requires exceptional strength.

18. Hiding behind a cloak of disorder is simply a question of subdivision; concealing courage under a a coat of timidity supposes a store of latent energy; masking strength with weakness is achieved with tactical dispositions.

A brief story illustrates this well. There was once a general who sent out spies to report on the condition of the enemy. The opposing general concealed his strong soldiers and well-nourished horses – only displaying emaciated donkeys to be seen. The spies then returned to report their findings to the general – with a recommendation to attack. All but one of the general's associates disagreed, saying: when two countries go to war, they naturally display as much strength as possible to deter the enemy from advancing, yet our spies have seen nothing but weakness, this is clearly some sort of trick and it would be unwise to attack. The general however did not heed the advice of his associate, fell in to the trap and found himself surrounded.

19. Therefore, a skilful general keeps the enemy moving by carefully creating a deceiving appearance, which the enemy will act upon.

A brief story illustrates this well. There was once a general with 100,000 soldiers, and ordered them to each create a fire. On the next evening he ordered half to create a fire, and on the first evening he ordered only a quarter to create a fire. Seeing this, the enemy believed the number of soldiers was decreasing each night and decided to pursue. The general calculated by the evening where their paths would intercept. He stripped a tree of its bark and inscribed on it: here my enemy will die. He then ordered his soldiers to fire shots if they were to see any light. The night fell and the enemy arrived, lighting a match to see what was inscribed on the tree. He then found himself riddled with shots and his whole army in total confusion.

20. By holding out bait, he keeps his enemy on the march; then waits with his soldiers for him.

21. The greatest of generals understands the effect of combined energy, and does not require too much from individuals.

A wise general first determines his army's total strength as a unit, then takes in to account talent of individual soldiers, and does not demand too much from the untalented. He is skilled in picking the right man for the right job.

22. When the general utilizes combined energy, his soldiers become like rolling stones downhill. As it is the nature of a stone to remain still on level ground. If it were a four-cornered object there will be no movement, but if round-shaped, to go rolling down.

23. Therefore, the energy developed by a unit of soldiers is like the momentum of a round stone rolled down a mountain thousands of feet in height.

The main lesson of this chapter is to utilise energy, combine troops, and to make swift and sudden movements.

CHAPTER 6 - WEAK AND STRONG POINTS

1. Whoever is first to battle awaits the enemy, and will be fresh for the fight; whoever is second has to rush and will arrive exhausted.

2. Therefore the greatest of generals impose their will on the enemy, and does not allow the enemy to impose theirs.

A great general will only fight on his own terms, or he does not fight at all.

3. By creating the impression of advantage to the enemy, he can cause the enemy to advance toward him; or by attacking, he can make it impossible for the enemy to come close.

A great general entices with bait, or strikes at a weak point which the enemy will have to defend.

4. If the enemy is resting, he can harass him; if well stocked with food, he can cut of routes to his supplies to starve him out; if based quietly, he can force him to move.

5. Appear in places which the enemy must defend; move swiftly to places where you are not expected to be.

6. An army may march great distances without distress, if it marches through country where the enemy is not.

Emerge from the void, like a bolt of lightning, strike at vulnerable points, ignore places that are well defended, attack in unexpected places.

7. You can be assured your attacks will succeed if you only attack places which are undefended. You can ensure your safety if you only hold positions that cannot be attacked.

The undefended points are the weak points, where the general lacks in capacity, or the soldiers lack spirit; where the walls are weak, or no precautions are taken; where aid will arrive too late, or supplies are light, or the defenders are not in co-operation with each other.

To have in penetrable defence, you must be able to defend even the points which are unlikely to be attacked and even more so those which are very likely to be attacked. A skilled warrior strikes from above like lightening making it impossible to defend against him. The general attacks the places the enemy cannot defend. A general who is highly skilled in defence hides in the most secret of recesses, making it impossible for the enemy to determine where he is. Therefore, a great general only holds positions which the enemy cannot attack.

8. Therefore a great general has great attacking skills when his enemy does not know what to defend, and great defence skills when his enemy does not know what to attack.

9. This divine art of elusiveness and concealment! By learning this skill, we can be invisible, and inaudible; and by doing so we can hold the enemy's fate in our hands.

10. You can attack and be overwhelming, if you strike the enemy's weak points; you can defend with ease if you make your movements more rapid than the enemy.

11. If we want to fight, we can force the enemy to fight, even if he's hiding somewhere. All we need do is attack another place that he will be obliged to defend.

If the enemy attacks, we can cut off his communication and occupy the roads which he has to use upon his return. If we are the attacking party – we shall go straight for the king.

12. If we do not wish to fight, we can prevent the enemy from advancing even if we are clearly visible. All we need do is to throw something strange and unexpected in his way.

Confuse the enemy with an unusual display and demeaner. A brief story illustrates this well: A general was about to be attacked, and so threw open his gates, stopped beating the war-drums and welcomed the enemy in. The enemy seeing this suspected it was a trap and turned away – which was the intended effect. This is the use of a bluff to defend.

13. Discover the enemy's positions, and keep your soldiers concentrated, and the enemy's must divide theirs.

If the enemy's positions are visible, we can attack him as one body; but if our positions are unknown, the enemy will be forced to divide his forces in order to guard against attacks from every possible direction.

14. We can be united as one body, while the enemy is forced to split into fractions. Therefore, there will be one whole against parts of a whole, which means we will always outnumber the enemy.

15. And when we attack an inferior force with our superior one, our opponents will be overpowered.

16. When we intend the battle we must not make the location known; because then the enemy will have to prepare against attacks at several different locations.

While some concern themselves with what you are going to do, focus mainly on what you are going to do. When the enemy divides his forces he is weaker at every point.

17. If the enemy strengthens his front, he weakens his rear; if he strengthens his front he weakens his rear, if he strengthens his left, he will weaken his right; if he strengthens his right, he will weaken his left. And If he sends his soldiers everywhere, he will be weak everywhere.

Being too defensive in war makes us less able to attack. Generals with little experience attempt to protect all points, but those who know the profession well, have their objective in mind, and only guard against significant blows, and will concede small misfortunes to avoid greater ones.

18. Weakness in terms of numbers comes from having to prepare against possible attacks; however, strength of numbers, comes from prompting the enemy to prepare in this manner for us.

Compel the enemy to scatter his forces, and then attack with superior forces at each point.

19. If we know the time and place of the battle, we can concentrate our forced from great distance.

The general calculates the distance of the battle, and develops a strategy which enables him to gather his soldiers for the purpose of a long and speedy march, and then at exactly the right moment and location he splits his army in to left and right wings in order to confront the enemy with overwhelming strength.

20. If the time and date are unknown, then the left wing will be powerless to aid the right, the right will be powerless to aid the left, the front unable to alleviate the rear, and the rear unable to support the front.

If the location and time of battle is unknown, the general is unable to concentrate his forces and must separate them to defend various points. This weakens his force, and leaves him vulnerable to superior attacks.

21. Although an enemy may have a greater number of soldiers, that will not guarantee their victory. Therefore, I say victory can still be achieved.

In the chapter on Tactical Dispositions it is said, 'One may know how to conquer without being able to do it,' yet here the statement is: 'victory can still be achieved'. In the preceding chapter on offense and defence, it is meant if the enemy is fully prepared, it cannot be a guaranteed victory, although one may know how to win. But 'victory can still be achieved', refers to soldiers without knowledge of the time and location of the battle.

22. The enemy may be stronger in numbers, but we can disrupt his attacks. Work to uncover his plan and the likelihood of its success.

Be sure to know all the plans that lead to your own success, and that of the enemy's downfall.

23. Shake him, force him to make a move, and observe if he is active or not.

Finding a method to shake the enemy allows to determine his position. Either seeking to lie low, or the opposite. This forces him to reveal himself, and display weak spots.

24. Carefully compare the enemy's army to your own, so you can determine its strengths and deficiencies.

25. When forming tactics, the highest form you can achieve is their complete concealment.

Concealment in this sense does not mean invisibility, like showing no signs or indications of what you intend to do, but conceal the tactics and you will find yourself safe from discreet spies, and the wisest minds. Even if the enemy has clever officers they will not be able to form any plans against yours.

26. To know how victory can be achieved from the enemy's own tactics that is what most cannot comprehend.

27. All men can see the tactics I have used to conquer, but none can see is the strategy from which victory has evolved.

It is easy to see after the battle, what methods were used to win, but what is not visible is the long series of plans and combinations developed long before the battle had begun.

28. Do not repeat the same tactics which gave you a victory, instead let your tactics by guided by an infinite variety of circumstances.

There is a foundational underpinning which leads to victory, yet the tactics which are used for it are infinite. The rules of strategy are simple and can be learned in a week. They can be taught with a few illustrations. But the knowledge of these does not make one a general – just as one with an understanding of grammar make one a great writer.

29. Military tactics are like water; as water naturally falls from high places and rushes downward.

30. Therefore, in war, the way is to avoid what is strong is to strike what is weak.

Seek the soft spots to attack and be like water, you will notice it does not struggle and flow uphill.

31. Water follows the ground which it flows over; the soldier plans his victory in relation to the enemy he faces.

32. Therefore, just as water is shapeless, in warfare there is no single set of conditions.

33. One who is able to modify his tactics to that of his enemy and succeed in winning, is a heaven sent general.

34. The five elements (water, fire, wood, metal and earth) are not always equally prevalent, there are short and long days, and the moon comes and goes.

This illustrates nothing is fixed, but even less so in war, as there is even less predictability than the elements, and the rotations of day and night.

CHAPTER 7 - MANAUVERING

1. In war, the general receives his commands from the King.

If you happen to be the general of your life, you are also the King. Give the commands to your inner general to execute.

2. After a King selects a general, and by proxy builds his army he must also harmonise various other aspects to allow the army to function properly

There must be harmony among the ranks of the army, and before any war can be formulated, there must also be harmony domestically within general society. Applying to a man who is a King and General combined, there also must be harmony within the household.

3. After this is tactical manoeuvring. This is the hardest part of warfare.

Once plans are formulated, the tactical manoeuvres become the hardest part of the war. The difficulty is to be found in finding favourable positions. Difficulties arise when seeking to turn indirect attacks in to direct, and troubles in to gains.

An example: make it appear you are far away, allow the enemy to relax, then move as fast as possible to appear where unexpected.

4. Therefore, a general facing a lengthy route, may draw an enemy toward another location, and then with him out the way take a more direct route and arrive before the enemy. This is the art of deviation.

5. Manoeuvring with a disciplined army is valuable; with an undisciplined group, it is the most dangerous.

Manoeuvres may be profitable or dangerous depending on the ability of the general to form a disciplined army.

6. If you order a fully equipped army to advance with a full load, you are more than likely to be late. On the other hand, to disperse your soldiers as fast as falcons for this purpose will require sacrifice of baggage and supplies.

If something requires action, there is a task to achieve, loading up all you need for the mission creates delay, and carrying everything with you will do the same. Sometimes what is required is to sacrifice the weights, and know you can't take everything with you, if you need to move fast.

7. Therefore, you can order your soldiers to advance without delay, day or night, covering double the usual distance in one go.

When traveling light, movements can be made rapidly. Never carry or store more than is required.

8. If you utilise one-hundred percent of your soldiers, with the strongest placed in front and the weaker ones at the rear,

there is potential that only one-tenth of your army to reach the destination.

An acknowledgement of the fact, that long campaigns bring about casualties, and that a lot of men can be lost by doing so, limits this type of rapid movement to surprise attacks which are absolutely necessary, and very infrequent.

9. If you advance with fifty percent of your soldiers to out manoeuvre the enemy, you may lose the leader of your first division, and only half of your force will reach the destination.

10. If you advance with thirty percent with the same objective, two-thirds of your army will arrive.

From these brief statements, you may ascertain the difficulty in manoeuvring large numbers of soldiers.

11. An army without baggage and supplies is lost.

If one deposits supplies at one location, and moves along without them is not technically lost, but operating away from base – and this would be for the purpose of rapid movement.

12. We can never form an alliance until we understand the plans of the other.

Alliances cannot be made unless two armies are in accord and have the same objectives.

13. We are not ready to lead an army to another country if we are not familiar with its terrain, its mountainous regions, forests, dangers, cliffs and swamps.

Navigation is made difficult without the study of maps and landscape. In any endeavour, you must seek to know the full extent of the landscape.

14. It is difficult to find and utilise natural advantages unless we find specific local information.

15. In war, practice disguise, and you will succeed.

Deceive enemies, especially in regards to your numerical strength.

16. Whether to concentrate or to divide your troops, must be decided by circumstances.

17. Let your rapidity be that of the wind.

Not only is the wind fast, but it is also invisible and leaves no tracks.

18. When attacking aggressively be like fire.

Be fierce like a blazing fire, as no man can stop this. When holding positions, and an enemy tries to remove you, or lure you away, be immovable like a mountain.

19. Your plans should be dark and impenetrable like night, so when you move, you appear like a thunderbolt.

You cannot close your ears to thunder, or your eyes from lightening. They are both unexpected. These cannot be prepared for or defended against.

20. When you conquer a countryside, let what is seized by divided amongst your soldiers.

This is not meant to mean abuse and take anything, it is intended to mean that the rewards of legitimate achievement shall be divided fairly between those who made the victory possible. In some cases, rewards are to be pooled together and drawn upon by all the soldiers in a proportionate manner.

Any land that is taken by the general and his soldiers should be utilised. The soldiers should plant and harvest. It is by this method – that more triumph is to come.

21. Consider all you can carefully before making a move.

A general and his soldiers should not move position before they have determined the power and intelligence of the enemy. This can be recapped in Chapter 1 – Laying Plans.

22. A general will win if he has learnt the art of deviation.

This is the art of manoeuvring.

24. Gongs and drums, banners and flags, are used to draw the enemy's ears and eyes to particular points.

If the sound and vision can be drawn to a single point, then no matter how many soldiers there are, they all focus in one direction like they are a single man.

25. By forming an army as a single united body, is it impossible for the brave to advance alone, or the cowardly to retreat alone.

A soldier should not advance or retreat against the orders of the general.

There was once a brave soldier that advanced alone, killed two of the enemy's soldiers and returned. The general had him beheaded. Others thought he deserved to live on account of his bravery. But no matter how brave it was, he was beheaded for acting without orders.

This is the art of handling large groups of men.

26. When fighting in darkness, make much use of fire and drums to influence the ears and eyes of the enemy, when fighting in day light, make use drums, flags and banners, to influence the ears and eyes of the enemy.

There was one a general that wanted to move at night with 500 soldiers, they made such noise and signs, that the enemy was forced to acknowledge their presence.

27. Rob the enemy's army spirit.

If a spirit of anger pervades all ranks of an army at one and the same time, its attack will be irresistible. The spirit of the enemy will be at its height upon arrival, this is therefore the cue not to fight, but to delay as much as possible until the enemy's spirit has calmed.

A general once heard the sound of the enemy's drums, and said 'this is not the moment to attack'. He then waited until the drums had sounded several times before finally giving orders to attack. They fought and won. Afterward he was asked why did he delay at first. He responded: 'on the first sounding of the drum the enemy's spirit is at its height, on the second it has faded, and on the third it is gone altogether. I decide to attack when their spirit had weakened and ours was at its height.

The first among the four most important influences of war is spirit. The value of a whole army can be influenced by one man alone. This is the power of spirit.

A commander-in-chief must possess spirit, but has to guard against being robbed of his presence of mind. His presence of mind is his most important asset. It is the quality which enables him to forge discipline and to inspire courage into those that fear.

Attacking does not only consist of attacking cities or striking the enemy's army in a battle; it also includes the art of assaulting the enemy's mental stability.

28. A soldier's spirit is strongest in the morning;

Breakfast, the most important meal of the day. At the battle of the Trebia, the Romans were unwisely allowed to fight without eating first, whereas Hannibal's men had a large breakfasted beforehand, by midday the Roman's energy had begun to decrease and by the evening, the general's mind was set on returning to base.

Fuel yourself before the fight, energy is required for exertion, and to deter hunger from becoming a distraction.

29. A wise general, therefore, avoids an army when its spirit is at its height, but attacks it when it is lethargic and motivated to retreat.

This is the art of studying moods.

30. Being disciplined and calm, and awaiting the appearance of disorder amongst the enemy is the art of retaining composure.

31. To achieve objectives while the enemy is still far from it, to be at peace while the enemy is struggling, to be well-nourished while the enemy is starving is the art of managing one's strength.

32. To refrain from attacking an enemy whose banners are in perfect order, to refrain from confronting an army which appears calm and confident is the art of studying circumstances.

33. It is a military truism never to advance uphill against the enemy, or to oppose him when he comes downhill.

34. Do not pursue an enemy who simulates his defeat; do not attack soldiers whose anger is intense.

35. Do not take the bait offered by the enemy.

Never take food or drink left by the enemy – as it likely tinted with poison. Never accept gifts from a known enemy.

Never intercept an enemy returning home. A man returning home will fight to the death against any attempt to hinder his journey, and is therefore a much too dangerous opponent at this point.

36. When you surround an army, leave an outlet free.

This does not literally mean leave an escape route, but only the appearance of one. If an enemy believes there is no escape he will fight with the courage of despair. Therefore, leave the appearance of a way out to avoid this, and after you can crush him. Never attack a desperate enemy. Peaceful animals will use their teeth and claws if cornered.

37. This is the art of warfare.

CHAPTER 8 - VARIATION OF TACTICS

1. In war, the general receives his commands from the King.

Repeated from the previous chapter, which emphasises that the King has ultimate control. The general executes the plans of the King.

2. When in a difficult country, do not set up a base. In country where high roads intersect, join forces with your allies. Never stay too long in dangerously isolated positions.

It is never wise to remain in a position with poor roads, without access to water, animals, vegetation or wood for fire. In our modern world, this would mean setting up home in a remote place, without access to any essentials for daily living.

In tight situations like this, you can only rely on stratagem, and if you find yourself in a desperate situation your only resort is to fight.

3. There are roads which must not be followed.

There are times its best not to attack, the pyrrhic victory is not worth it. As much as you may want to, as much as you may feel obliged to, if the victory leads to huge depletion of time, energy, and resources, it is not worth it. It is also useless to attempt to win a small battle, whereby if you triumph you gain very little, but if you lose, make yourself a laughing stock. Avoid pyrrhic victories.

4. A general who completely understands the advantages that accompany variation of tactics knows how to handle his soldiers.

5. The general who does not understand these, may understand the terrain of the country, but he will not be able to turn his knowledge in to a practical gain.

This literally means being able to get the most out of the ground, and using all the natural advantages of it as possible.

There are various types of terrain, or arenas to enter, but how is it possible to do your best, if it is not supplemented by a versatility of mind?

6. Therefore, a student of war who is inexperienced in the art and varying his plans, even though he may understand the Five Advantages, will fail to make the best use of his soldiers.

The five advantages:

1. If a road is short, it must be followed.
2. if an army is isolated, it must be attacked.
3. if a town is in an unsafe condition, it must be sieged.
4. if a position can be captured, it must be attempted.

5. If consistent with military operations, the ruler's commands must be obeyed.

However, there are occasions where these advantages should not be taken. For example: a particular road may be the shortest, but if the general knows that it is full of natural obstacles, or that the enemy is plotting to attack there, he will not travel that road. The enemy may be open to attack, but the general knows his backs against the wall and will fight with desperation, he will refrain from the attack.

7. Therefore, in a superior general's plans, considerations of advantage and disadvantage will be included.

When in an advantageous position or disadvantageous one, the opposite scenario should be present in your mind.

8. If our expectation of an advantageous position be moderated in this manner, we can succeed in accomplishing the essential part of our plans.

Never expect complete advantage, always factor in the enemy doing damage and factor it into calculations.

9. And if on the other hand, while finding ourselves in difficulty we must be ready to take advantage of opportunities which will lift us out of misfortune.

To take oneself out of dangerous positions, it is important to factor in the enemy's ability to do damage, but be fully aware of your own ability to take advantage. If these two guidelines are followed one will be liberated.

An example: A general finding himself surrounded by the enemy, only thinking of escape, will encourage the enemy to attack and destroy. But if a general launches a bold counter attack, he can use the advantage gained to free himself.

10. Reduce the hostile enemies by inflicting damage to them.

Various methods to inflict damage consist of:

- *Luring the enemy's most trusted advisors away so he is left without good advice.*
- *Introduce traitors into his administration so his policies are affected.*
- *Provoke deceit to create dissension among a general and soldiers.*
- *Cause the weakening of his people, and waste of resources.*
- *Corrupt the enemy's morals by delivering luxurious gifts which lead him into excess.*
- *Disturb his focus by presenting attractive women.*
- *Create positions for the enemy to enter, where he must suffer damage.*
- *Cause trouble for the enemy's assets, the currency, the synchronisation of his soldiers, and their loyalty to him.*
- *Prevent any rest.*
- *Present enticements to make him forget any previous natural impulse, and subsequently lure him to a given point.*

11. The art of war teaches us not to rely on the enemy not coming, but on us being ready for him. The art of war teaches us not to rely on a chance of no attack, but on making our position unassailable.

12. There are five dangerous faults which may affect a general:

1 - Recklessness, which leads to destruction.

Being brave without careful deliberation causes a man to fight blindly. An opponent like this should not be met with force, but lured, like a mad bull chasing a red flag, into a position where he can be trapped and destroyed.

Never take solely into account an enemy's courage while forgetting this is only one attribute of a great general. A general with this attribute alone, who fights recklessly should be condemned.

Simply rushing to one's death does not equal victory.

2 - Cowardice, which leads to capture.

Never be a man who will not take initiative to gain advantage. Never be one is quick to run away from anything dangerous. Never be one who is only concerned with returning alive – a man like this will never take a risk. Nothing can be achieved in war without taking risks. Those that always let advantages slip away, will eventually bring their own disaster.

A brief story illustrates: there once was a general that kept a small boat in the river as an escape route. The natural result of this was his soldier's fighting spirit was weakened, they were then attacked with such force that they were forced to burn their supplies and fled on the boat for two days.

3 – Being quick to anger, which can be provoked by insults.

A brief story illustrates: there once was a general that was easily angered, his enemy was well aware, and so plotted to continuously attack his walls. His assumption being that the general inside would be very angry and come out to attack – whereby he would be an easy target to destroy. The plan was acted upon, the general came out was lured as far as the enemy's men had retreated to, and then he was attacked and destroyed.

4 – A feeling of honour which is sensitive to shame.

This is not intended to mean having honour is a defect found in a general, but is rather meant to mean being overly sensitive to attacks against this honour. Being a thin-skinned general, who is easily stung by insults, deserved or not, is not conducive for victory. The seeker of glory should be careless of public opinion.

5 – Too much care for his soldiers, which exposes him to worry and trouble.

This again does not mean that a general should have no care or consideration for his soldiers. This means that the general at times will have to sacrifice the comfort of himself and soldiers for significant military operations for the advantage they bring to him and his men.

The general must have his eyes on victory, because his soldiers will suffer more from defeat than temporary discomfort. A general cannot let his compassion allow him to release a captured city, or relieve his soldiers if it is contrary to his better judgment. A great general must place what is best for the whole, above what is best for a segment.

13. These are the five greatest sins of a general, which are disastrous to the conduct of war.

14. When an army is destroyed and its general murdered, the cause will be found as one of these five dangerous faults.

Meditate on them.

CHAPTER 9 -AN ARMY ON THE MARCH

1. When positioning the army, and observing signs of the enemy, pass quickly over mountains, and stay in the region of valleys.

Stay in locations that can provide for the army, natural resources and water, barren lands are to be avoided.

A brief story illustrates: there once was a general that knew to stay close to valleys, his opponent did not. The general secured all positions with water and plants. His opponent finding himself and his army growing weak due to lack of supplies eventually surrendered.

2. Camp in high places, not in mountains but on small hills, elevated above the local area facing the sun.

Do not climb mountains to fight, avoid warfare from above.

3. After crossing a river, appear far away from it.

If you wish your enemy to cross the same river, appear as far away from it as possible. This will temp your enemy to cross as well.

4. When the enemy crosses the river, do not advance to attack in mid-stream. It is best to let half the army across, and then deliver your attack.

By attacking half of the enemy's army mid-stream allows the other half to survive. By allowing half of the enemy's army to cross, you can annihilate them, and then attack the other half mid-stream. Totally wiping them out.

5. If you fear the fight, do not advance to meet the enemy near a river in an attempt to prevent him crossing.

6. Position your boat higher the stream than the enemy, facing the sun. Never move up-stream to meet the enemy.

An enemy that positions himself higher up the stream may poison the water, or dam the stream, and then release a flood.

7. When crossing marshes, your main concern should be to pass quickly, without any delay.

Marshes have poor quality water, are flat, open and expose you to attack.

8. If you are forced to fight in marsh, you should have your back to trees.

The trees will serve as a defence to the rear, and generally where there are trees the ground is more secure.

9. On dry level ground, position yourself with a stream to one side, and rising ground to one side and rear.

Being positioned like this, the attacks can only come from the front, and the army is secure from unexpected side attacks.

10. These are the four useful branches of military knowledge

1. Mountains.
2. Rivers.
3. Marshes.
4. Plains (level ground).

11. All armies prefer high ground to low.

Higher ground is advantageous, that which is low is usually dark and damp. From above the army has a clearer view.

12. If you care for your men, provide them with fresh water and food, and set up camp on solid ground. By doing so your soldiers will avoid disease.

Nourishment, and a dry climate eradicate disease. Stay well-nourished and seek sunshine.

13. When you arrive at the base of hill or a bank, take the sunny side, with the slope on your right rear. Doing so, your soldiers will benefit from utilising the natural advantages of the ground.

14. When heavy rain causes overflow to a river you wish to cross, you have to wait until it subsides.

15. Do not stay on land with dangerous cliffs and torrents of water that rush along streams. Avoid confined spaces that appear to be natural prisons, easy to get into but hard to get out of. Avoid unstable ground, and heavy mud as vehicles and soldiers will not move easily.

16. While we avoid these places, entice the enemy to approach them; while we face him, and make the enemy have them behind him.

17. Be on our guard against traitors, covert enemies, secretly spying for our weaknesses and listening to our instructions.

18. When the enemy is close yet remains quiet, he is relying on the natural strength of his position.

19. When the enemy is aloof and tries to provoke a battle, he is anxious for the other side to advance.

When the enemy tries to provoke us, he realises the strength of our position and seeks to dislodge us for his advantage.

20. If his location is easily accessible, he is trying to lure us toward him.

21. Movement amongst the trees indicates that the enemy is advancing.

Send scouts to climb trees and look out for movement. Essentially use your own spies to see if the enemy is advancing. However, too much movement means the enemy wants us to be aware – and this can be a trap. No movement at all can indicate the enemy has fled and fears pursuit, however it can also be a lure for us to advance.

22. The rising of birds in their flight is the sign of an attack.

When birds are flying in a straight formation, and suddenly shoot upwards, it indicates the soldiers have moved rapidly underneath the birds' location.

23. When dust rises upward, it is the sign of vehicles approaching; when remains low but spreads across a wide area it indicates soldiers advancing.

Stay vigilant for indirect signs of enemy movement.

24. Kind words and an increase in preparation is a signal that the enemy may be about to advance. Offensive language and rushing forward to attack are signs that he will retreat.

Paradoxically when one is kind, but also appears to be increasing their preparations -they may actually be masking a threat, but one who is actively aggressive and confrontational, may actually be masking a weakness.

25. When the light vehicles become visible and take positions at the side lines, it signifies the enemy is preparing for battle.

Watch for subtle indications of the enemy trying to prepare for battle discreetly.

26. When one proposes peace, without drawing up a formal contract, indicates a plan.

If an enemy wishes to cease the war, without adding to it any reasons and formal proposals, this may indicate deception for you to lower your guard.

27. When the soldiers rush in to place and take formation under their banner, it means the moment has arrived.

Strong formation indicates an inclination to advance, preparation has been complete and the soldiers are ready.

28. When soldiers are seen to be advancing and then retreating, it is a lure.

A strong army, in appropriate formation does not attack to retreat, especially without justification. If this appears to be the case, it is a scheme devised to entice one in to a trap.

29. When the soldiers are not seen to be standing upright, they are weak from lack of food.

The weak and feeble have bad posture, where they are seen to be slouching and not carrying themselves appropriately – it indicates either poor self-care, strong fatigue or lack of food.

30. If soldiers are sent to collect water and immediately begin drinking before they return, the army is suffering from thirst.

As an army is a collective of men, it is possible to determine the condition of the army by observing a single man. If a soldier does not have patience when awaiting their food and water, they are suffering from lack of supplies. This is important to note, because not only does it apply to the enemy, it can apply to any general and his soldiers.

31. If the enemy has an opportunity to take advantage but doesn't, his soldiers are exhausted.

If one does not take opportunities as they are presented, it usually is an indication of fear or fatigue, in this case a general should have training rigorously to eliminate fear, and all that can remain is fatigue.

32. If birds gather in a particular location, it is unoccupied.

That which is easily disturbed will not congregate in places of high activity.

33. If there is commotion between the soldiers, the general's authority is weak. If the soldiers are angry, it means that the men are fatigued.

The soldiers become angry based upon the level of demand placed upon them and how tired they become. Never over work the soldiers where it can be avoided, but also never let them become slack.

34. When an army deliberately exhausts their total supply of food, and packs their tents away, you know they do not intent to return and are prepared to fight to the death.

35. When soldiers are whispering together in small groups this indicates separation amongst the men.

36. When a general is giving rewards too frequently it indicates he is coming to an end of his resources.

Frequent gifts signify the general distrusts his men, and is attempting to pacify their growing hostility toward him. His power is waning – and soon his resources will be depleted.

37. To begin without calculation, and afterward fear the enemy's numbers, shows the highest lack of intelligence.

38. When the enemy sends compliments, it can indicate that the enemy wants a truce.

If an enemy opens friendly negotiations, for example offers to return hostages in exchange for something – they are usually seeking a resolution. There is usually a reason backing this, such as lack of recourses or strength.

39. If the enemy's soldiers advance furiously but then remain for a long time without starting a battle or retreating, the situation demands great vigilance.

This type of manoeuvre at times is used as a diversionary tactic while an attack is launched elsewhere.

40. If our soldiers are of the same quantity as the enemy that is sufficient, but it means no direct frontal attacks should be made.

If equally matched, never meet head on, device a strategy to launch an indirect attack or take time to build greater strength.

41. A general who takes no precautions and underestimates his enemy is sure to be beaten by them.

If a bee can sting, and a scorpion can kill, never under estimate an enemy no matter how small he appears to be.

42. If soldiers are punished before they have accepted you as their leader, they will not submit; and, unless they submit they will be practically useless to you. If, when the soldiers have accepted you are their leader, punishments are not administered, they will still be useless.

43. Therefore, soldiers must be treated at first with compassion, but kept under control with iron discipline.

The ideal leader combines hard with soft, discipline with kindness. Leading in this manner paves the way for victory.

44. If the soldiers' commands are routinely enforced, the army will be a well-disciplined machine; if not, its discipline will be weak.

45. A general cannot show a lack of confidence in his men, and then always expect they obey his orders.

If a general has confidence in his men, the respect will be mutual. The general should have confidence in his men, so that when the time comes they will respect his orders and their discipline will be maintained – because they all trust and look up to him.

Never take too long rectifying petty mistakes, or be led by minor doubts. Being pedantic and unsure is the path to losing your soldiers' confidence.

CHAPTER 10 - TERRAIN

1. There are six types of terrain:

(1) Accessible ground.

Abundant with roads and communication tools.

(2) Entangling ground.

Areas in which, if you enter, you become entangled.

(3) Temporizing ground.

Ground which allows you to create a delay.

(4) Narrow passes.

(5) Steep heights.

(6) Positions at a great distance from the enemy.

4,5 & 6: are self-explanatory.

2. Ground which can be freely navigated by both sides is called: Accessible.

Areas which the general and his enemy can freely enter – is an access point to battle.

3. In regards to accessible ground ensure to arrive before the enemy and occupy the best spots, and carefully guard your line of supplies.

If one location is accessible – arrive first, in this way you can position yourself to have the advantage. You can also guard your supplies to the access point before the enemy takes positions which hinder this. Whoever arrives late will have less time to prepare, and will find himself taking weaker positions, and have his communication and supply lines affected by this. He may find himself dividing his army, and his defeat will not be ordinary, it may be his total ruin and surrender.

4. Ground which can be entered into freely, but harder to return from is called: entangling

5. From this sort of position, if the enemy unprepared, you may advance and defeat him. But if the enemy is prepared for you, and you fail to defeat him, and a retreat is impossible, it will be your disaster.

6. Positions that would create no gain for either side if they move, is called: temporizing ground.

In such locations, neither side finds it convenient to move and therefore the situation remains gridlocked.

7. In this type of position, even if the enemy offered attractive bait, we should not move, this is a lure which aims to induce us to change position.

it is advisable not to advance, but instead simulate retreat, turning the enticement back on the enemy, then, when his army emerges, we will attack with an advantage.

8. In regard to narrow passes, if you can arrive and position yourself first, heavily guard the entrance point with artillery, and wait for the enemy.

The general should take the initiative and being able to make sudden and unexpected attacks the enemy will have no chance.

9. If the enemy arrives first, do not follow him, only if you are certain the entrance point is weakly defended.

10. In regard to steep heights, if you arrive before the enemy, you will be able to take the elevated and sunny spots, and there you can await his coming.

The advantage of arriving at narrow passes or heights ensures that your movements cannot be dictated by the enemy. Taking elevated sunny positions not only allows an advantage when fighting, but also against the elements, rain can easily flood trenches.

11. If the enemy arrives before you, do not follow him, but retreat and try to entice him toward you.

12. If you are positioned a great distance from the enemy, and the strength of the two armies is equal, it is not easy to provoke a battle.

By keeping a large distance from the enemy, any army which travels to the other for the purpose of battle will exhaust tremendous amounts of energy while the other remains fresh and prepared. This is based upon the assumption that both armies are equally strong, because if one is significantly weak – travelling for the stronger army will not have too much impact on the ability to win.

13. These are the six principles relating to the ground:

Any general must study them.

14. An army can be exposed to six disasters, not arising from natural causes, but from faults which the general takes responsibility for.

These are:

1. Flight.
2. Insubordination.
3. Collapse.
4. Ruin.
5. Disorganization.
6. Rout.

15. If all other conditions are equal, and one army is thrown against another ten times its size, the result will be the flight.

16. When the soldiers are too strong and their leaders are too weak, the result is insubordination.

A brief story illustrates: There was once a general who was sent to lead a war, but the whole time his soldiers treated him with disapproval, riding around the camp on donkeys and laughing at him – he was powerless to stop this conduct. When the time for battle came, and he attempted to engage the enemy his soldiers scattered in all directions. After this humiliation the unlucky man committed suicide by cutting his throat.

When the leaders are too strong and the soldiers are too weak, the result is collapse.

This occurs when the officers are strong and eager to progress but the soldiers are too weak and lifeless to advance. This results in collapse.

17. When the higher officers are insubordinate to their general, and when encountering the enemy initiate battle themselves, from a feeling of anger and resentment, before the commander-in-chief has given an account whether or not they are in a position to fight, the result is ruin.

This occurs when the general is angry without cause and does not appreciate his officers, and therefore arouses intense resentment, which results in ruin for him.

18. When the general is weak and lacks authority; when his orders are not clear and distinct; his officers and soldiers

have no regular routine and lack formation; the result is total disorganisation.

When a general is decisive and gives orders without hesitation, the soldiers will not wait to hear again, but if his orders are given in an indecisive manner, the soldiers will not be clear about doing their duty. The secret to having orders followed successfully by the soldiers, can be found in the clarity of the instructions they receive. A most serious defect is indecision.

19. When a general, is unable to estimate the enemy's strength, and allows an inferior force to advance against it, or despatches a weak taskforce against a powerful one, and fails to place the right soldiers on the front line, the result is rout.

The keenness men have to be placed at the front, one to strengthen the spirit of those behind, and also to discourage the enemy.

20. These are the six ways a general can be defeated, which must be carefully studied by any general who has attained the position.

21. The natural formation of the country is the soldier's best ally.

The advantages and disadvantages of the weather and season are not equal to those in relation to the ground. The power of estimating the enemy, controlling the forces which lead to victory, and intelligently calculating difficulties, risks and distance, is the utmost test of a great general.

22. A general who knows these things, and puts his knowledge into practice, will win his battles. One who neigher knows, or does not practices them, will unquestionably be defeated.

23. If a battle will surely lead to victory, then you must fight, even if forbidden by the sovereign; if a battle is sure to result in defeat, then you must not fight even if the sovereign demands it.

The final decision rests with the general. This authority must be understood even by an enlightened monarch. The general's decision is absolute and not tainted by demands from above.

24. The general who goes forward without seeking fame and retreats without fearing dishonour, whose only thought is to defend his country and render useful service for his sovereign, is the jewel of the kingdom.

The hardest thing for a soldier to do is retreat. A true warrior is one who even if he had to suffer punishment would not regret his decisions.

25. Treat your soldiers as dear as your children, and they will follow you anywhere, into the depths, and through the hardest of times; treated them as treasured sons, and they will stand by your side to the death.

A brief story illustrates: There was once a soldier suffering from an abscess, his general came and sucked the poison out himself. After which, the soldier's mother began to cry. When asked why? She replied: 'many years ago, the general did the same for my husband, and after he never left his side, until one day he met his death during a battle, now my son will do the same'.

26. If, however, you are too lenient, and unable to make your authority felt; too kind-hearted, and unable to enforce your commands; and additionally, incapable of controlling disorder: then your soldiers are like spoilt children; and are useless for any practical purpose.

If your soldiers fear your discipline, they will not fear the enemy.

A brief story illustrates: There once was a general who ordered that nothing be taken from the inhabitants of a captured village. One soldier however, took it upon himself to take a hat from a local townsman to protect his head from the rain. The general, not one to tolerate a breach of direct orders, arranged his execution. The other soldiers were present to watch, and from that time on, not even an item left in the street was picked up.

27. If we know our soldiers are fully prepared to attack, but we do not know if the enemy is ready or not, we are only halfway towards victory.

A general's best position is to know both sides.

28. If we know that the enemy is prepared to attack, but are unsure if our soldiers are prepared, we are only halfway towards victory.

29. If we know that the enemy is prepared to attack, and also know that our soldiers are prepared, but we are unaware that the ground is impractical for fighting, we are only halfway towards victory.

30. Therefore the experienced general, once advancing, is never disoriented; once he has set the soldiers in motion, he will never lose.

A great general has taken all measures to ensure victory beforehand. He will never move thoughtlessly. So, when he moves he will make no mistake.

31. Therefore: If you know yourself and know the enemy, your victory will not be doubtful; and if you know the ground, your victory is complete.

Knowing these things, complete the three sides to the triangle of victory.

CHAPTER 11 - THE NINE SITUATIONS

1. The art of war recognizes nine types of ground:

    1. Dispersive ground.
    2. Facile ground.
    3. Contentious ground.
    4. Open ground.
    5. Ground of intersecting highways.
    6. Serious ground.
    7. Difficult ground.
    8. Hemmed-in ground.
    9. Desperate ground.

2. When a general has a battle in his own territory, it is called: dispersive ground.

Soldiers too close to home, their wives and children, are likely to disperse when things get tough. They will not fight with desperation, being too close to home makes them seek easy refuge.

3. When a general enters hostile territory, but no great distance in to it, it is called: facile ground.

This type of position leaves the option of returning on the table. It is said that when a general enters enemy ground, he should burn the boats or bridges to signify to all the soldiers there us not turning back.

4. Ground that offers great advantage to either side, is called: contentious ground.

This is ground which should be contended for, ground on which, whoever occupies has significant advantage over the enemy, such as a narrow passage: where an army can fight in the ratio of 1 man to 10.

5. Ground on which each side has total freedom of movement is called: open ground.

Ground on which supplies and communication tools can be operated with ease.

6. Ground which forms the key to three connecting states.

Ground which adjoins the enemy but also a third country. The general who occupies this position first has greater chance to compel the third country to become his ally.

7. When an army ventures in to the heart of enemy territory, leaving a number of secure locations behind, it is called: serious ground.

At this point the situation is serious.

8. Forests, steep mountains, marshes, and all ground that is difficult to traverse is called: difficult ground.

9. Ground which can only be reached by taking dangerous paths and difficult to navigate any form of escape, which mean a small number of the enemy could take out a large number of our soldiers is called: hemmed in ground.

10. Ground on which our survival relies on fighting without delay is called: desperate ground.

This is very similar to hemmed-in ground yet at this point there is no possible escape at all. Staying on desperate ground is like being in a leaking boat, or riding a burning horse.

An example would be falling in to an enemy trap. The enemy overwhelms us and suddenly appears. Our only option is to retreat.

11. On dispersive ground, therefore, do not fight. On facile ground, do not stop. On contentious ground, do not attack.

The main thing in these scenarios is to focus your energy on securing the advantageous position first.

12. On open ground, do not try to block the enemy's way.

An attempt to block the enemy in this scenario would be futile to your own.

Where countries intersect form alliances with neighbours.

13. On serious ground, do not abuse the local people.

When deep in enemy territory one must not abuse the general citizens, as it would be of more advantage for them to welcome your presence, perhaps working with you rather than against you.

When on difficult ground, keep moving forward.

14. On hemmed-in ground, resort to stratagem.

A brief story illustrates: A general finding himself hemmed-in waited until night fall. He then strapped to 2000 oxen bundles of twigs and set these alight. The bewildered animals rushed toward an area where the enemy had set up camp. The enemy being so startled by the strange moving objects lit up at night, decided to retreat, therefore making a clear path for the general to escape.

When on desperate ground, fight.

If you fight with all you have, there is a chance of survival, but if you freeze and give up, you will surely lose.

15. The skilful general knows how to drive separation between the enemy's front and rear.

Essentially a good general will find ways to create distance between the enemy's factions, in-turn limiting their communication with each other, and their ability to assist and support one another.

16. When the enemy's men are united, create disorder.

17. When it is advantageous, move forward, otherwise stay still.

18. When asked how to deal with a very organised enemy in on the verge of attack, I say: "start by taking something valuable to him, and then he will bend to your will."

The enemy has three objectives in mind when attacking:

1. To acquire our favourable positions.
2. To destroy our cultivated land.
3. To disturb ours, while guarding his own communications.

Our objective therefore would be to impede his plans, and by doing so you instantly place him in the defensive position.

19. Speed is the essence of war.

A brief story illustrates: there was a general who was discussing deserting his post and country for enemy land, and another general who found out about the treason, he immediately set off with an army to impede his plans. The general did not hesitate to make his move. His speed was such that within eight days he had arrived. The enemy believed that when the news of his departure reached anyone it would take a whole month before anyone appeared. Two weeks later the enemy lost his head.

20. The further you penetrate into enemy territory, the greater will be the solidarity of your soldiers, and therefore the defenders will not be able to overcome you.

21. Make short detours into fertile land in order to supply your soldiers with food.

22. Pay close attention to the welfare of your soldiers.

Entertain them, feed them well, look after them generally. Do not over-exhaust them. Concentrate their energy and reserve your strength.

A brief story illustrates: there was a general who anticipating an attack – decided to stay for a day behind his walls looking after his men, he provided them with meals, sharing his own food with them, he provided bathing facilities, and exercise areas – welding them into a concentrated force. When he believed they had heightened spirits and were ready for the battle, he opened his gates and upon seeing his soldiers rush forward the enemy retreated. Only to be found later and slaughtered.

Keep your army continually on the move.

By doing so the enemy can never know your whereabouts. Devise unfathomable plans.

23. Put your soldiers into positions which leave no escape, as naturally they would prefer to run than face death. However, if will face death, there is nothing they cannot achieve.

If one man runs into a town wielding a machete, and everybody else disperses, it would not mean that this man alone had courage and the rest were cowards. The truth is, a desperado and a man who places some value on his life do not meet on equal terms.

If soldiers are placed in an awkward position – they will unite and exert all possible strength to escape.

24. When soldiers are put in a position of no escape they will lose all sense of fear. When there is nowhere to turn, they will stand strong. If they are in hostile territory, they will show an immovable disposition. If there is no help or support, they will fight hard.

25. Therefore, without waiting to be positioned, the soldiers will be constantly be in formation; without waiting to be asked, they will execute your orders.

When soldiers are placed in a dire situation, they will essentially act your will without being asked to. Without any restrictions they will be faithful, without giving them any orders they can be trusted.

26. Never pay attention to those who say they can prophesise the future, and remove superstitious doubts. Then, unless death itself comes, no tragedy is to be feared.

When one is lost in doubt and fear, they degenerate into cowards and die a thousand times before their death. Never give in to superstition as this will destroy the presence of mind in the soldiers. Without doubt, and without fear, the soldiers' resolve will never waver until death.

27. If the soldiers are not overwhelmed with money, it is not because they despise riches; if their lives are not long, it is not because they dislike longevity.

If soldiers disregard money, or long life, it is not because they do not want these things, it is because they do not have a choice. A general must ensure that anything which leads the soldiers to evade fighting, is removed from their paths.

28. When the day of the battle arrives, the soldiers may weep.

This is not intended to say the soldiers should be allowed to cry because they are afraid. These tears are permitted to display the soldier's willingness to die.

29. The skilful tactician may be likened to a snake that is found in the mountains.

The mountain snake is both sudden and rapid. The general can if he wishes execute manoeuvres in the same manner. Try to strike the head, and you will be attacked by the tail. Try to attack the tail and you will be attacked by the head. Attack the middle and you will be attacked by both the head and tail.

30. Can an army can be made to imitate the mountain snake? Is it possible to make the front and rear of an army swiftly respond to an attack on the other, as if they were both part of a single living body?

Yes, just as the left hand helps the right.

31. It is not enough to put one's trust in the soldiers after forcing them to stay put by use of mechanical means.

For example, you cannot hide fuel for vehicles and then trust that the army will not move. Your soldiers must have a unified purpose, and spirit of cooperation.

32. Set up one standard of courage which all must reach.

A standard of courage must be made which all soldiers must aim for and eventually reach, and one standard must be set that no one can fall below.

33. How to utilise the strong and weak, is a question that pertains to the appropriate use of ground.

Strong positions must be given to the weaker, as they can hold out longer here. And more exposed positions should be given to the stronger. This balances out the differences in strength. There are immense benefits to be discovered when studying and applying the knowledge of correct positioning.

34. Therefore, the skilful general conducts his army as if he were leading a single man.

Not only does this apply to the way in which he leads, but also how easily he does it.

35. It is the responsibility of a general to be quiet and ensure secrecy; remain upright, and maintain order.

36. He must be able to confuse his officers and soldiers with false reports and appearances, keeping them in total ignorance when necessary.

The soldiers must not be allowed to form part of the strategizing process, they are only allowed to celebrate the successful outcomes. Puzzling and surprising the enemy is standard practise, but why do this to your own men?

A brief story illustrates: there was a general that found himself outnumbered, and ordered most of his men to divide in all directions. He said the enemy is heading east and I will head west with 8,000 men. The enemy got wind of his plans, and headed west to block the generals retreat. Yet the general really had begun to head east with his men to intercept the enemy. The general later found the enemy encamped and attacked them at night, most retreated in utter confusion, yet the general returned with 5,000 heads as trophies and all of the enemy's belongings. In this case we see that the general had concealed his real plans from his men, and made a bold move when dividing his army in order to deceive the enemy,

37. When a general constantly readapts his plans and strategy, he keeps the enemy without definite knowledge.

Deception is necessary in war, not only the deception of the enemy but of your own soldiers. They must be willing to follow you without knowing why. By shifting position and taking indirect routes, the general prevents the enemy from anticipating his moves.

38. During critical times, the leader of an army acts like one who has climbed a ladder and then kicks it away to the floor. He takes his soldiers deep into enemy territory before he reveals why.

The general must be willing to take decisive steps which make it impossible for the soldiers to return. This will put all soldiers fully under your command.

39. A general burns his boats, and acts like a shepherd leading a flock of sheep, he drives his men while they have no idea where he is going.

The army should only be acquainted with the orders to attack, defend or retreat, and remain ignorant to the ulterior motives.

40. To assemble his soldiers and lead them into danger is the business of a general.

A general must be able to lead his soldiers into dangerous places and then be willing to strike the enemy hard. The desertion of soldiers must be considered in war, however a true general can lead without his soldiers deserting.

41. A general must study the different measures suited to the nine varieties of ground; the practicality of aggressive or defensive tactics; and the fundamental laws of human nature.

42. When invading enemy territory, the general rule is: that penetrating deeply brings unity to the army; penetrating only a little bit can lead to dispersion.

43. When you leave your country and enter an enemy land, you find yourself on critical ground.

Critical ground is that which is not advanced enough to become: facile, and not so short that it is: dispersive. It lies somewhere in the middle and is of very rare occurrence.

44. When you enter deep into enemy territory, it is serious ground. When you penetrate only a little bit, it is facile ground.

45. When the enemy occupies strong positions behind you and there are very narrow passages in front, it is hemmed-in ground. When there is no place of refuge or retreat, it is desperate ground.

46. Therefore, when on dispersive ground, the general inspires his men with unity of purpose.

On facile ground, a general will ensure that there is strong cohesion between all parts of the army.

This is to guard against two possibilities:

1. *The desertion of soldiers.*
2. *A sudden attack from the enemy.*

47. On contentious ground, the general speeds up the rear.

The general speeds up the rear to bring it closer to the head, so that the head and tail reach the desired destination together. The rear must not be allowed to straggle behind.

48. On open ground, a general carefully considers his defence. On ground of intersecting paths, the general consolidates with his alliances.

49. On serious ground, the general aims to ensure a continuous stream of supplies.

On difficult ground, the general keeps pushing the soldiers forward along the road.

50. On hemmed-in ground, the general blocks any form of retreat.

The general's intention is to imply he intends to defend the position he is in, but his real intention is to suddenly attack. This is to cause the soldiers to fight with desperation – and not allow them to be inclined to run away.

On desperate ground, the general declares to his soldiers the hopelessness of them escaping alive.

The general then proceeds to destroy all supplies, and provisions, and makes it very clear that now is the time to fight or die. The only chance of life is to give up all hope of it.

51. It is the soldier's disposition to offer relentless resistance when surrounded, to fight fully when he fears for his life, and to obey promptly all orders when in danger.

52. We can never form an alliance until we understand the plans of the other.

Some sentences are repeated to emphasize their importance.

53. To ignore of any one of the preceding or following principles does not suit a warlike general.

54. When a warlike general launches an attack on a powerful state, his leadership shows itself in preventing the concentration of the enemy's forces. He overpowers his opponents, and their allies are deterred from turning against him.

When attacking, the general seeks to divide the enemy's forces and concentrate his own, giving him the superiority of strength. This will overpower the enemy and any country which has formed an alliance with the general will be frightened to switch sides.

55. Therefore, he does not strive to ally himself with all and harness the power of others. He carries out his own secret plans, and keeps his enemies in awe.

With superior strength he can afford not to form all alliances, and simply execute his secret plans. His prestige will enable him to cut off external friendships when necessary.

56. Give rewards to the brave and punish the cowardly.

Final instructions to the soldiers should not be like any before. Never reveal your plans beforehand. Orders should be flexible and a great general has to have the willingness to entirely switch strategies in a moment's notice. By doing so a general will handle the whole army as if it were a single man. Reward the soldiers' good deeds when recognised, and ensure to discipline cowardly soldiers.

57. Give your soldiers the final order; never let them know the entire plan.

Never spend time explaining the reasoning behind the order. Give no reason for decisions. This applies as much as it does to a general as it does to a judge.

58. Place your army in a fatal position, and it will survive; lead it through a hopeless passage, and it will come out safely.

The human spirit is immeasurably powerful, and can face tremendous adversity. In fact, that which appears to have the power to break us, to cause great pain and suffering – can do nothing to us. On the contrary, by going through dark and difficult times one becomes stronger, and when the spirit is placed into a position of difficulty – it will do all it can to survive.

59. When an army finds itself in harm's way it is fully capable of delivering the finishing blow for victory.

Danger stimulates men to do the impossible.

60. Success in warfare is gained by accepting and working with the enemy's purpose.

Appear to yield to the enemy. If the enemy advances, lead him on to do so. If the enemy wishes to withdraw, give space. By doing so – he will become thoughtless, and carefree. Then deliver the attack.

61. By persistently following the enemy, and uniting our forces, we will succeed in killing the commander-in-chief.

62. This is the ability to succeed with absolute cunning.

63. The day you take command, secure the borders, destroy all previous records, and halt the movement of all ambassadors to or from enemy countries.

64. Be unyielding in meetings.

Do not show weakness, insist your plans be followed, and control the situation – and ensure secrecy of any negotiations.

65. If an enemy leaves a door open, rush through.

Provided it was not intentionally left open as a trap.

This is meant to mean if the enemy is careless and provides a genuine opportunity for you to take advantage - you should do so.

66. Control your opponent's moves by capturing what he holds dear, and then carefully determine the time of his arrival.

By acquiring a favourable position, it is not guaranteed to be turned in to an advantage, simply because the enemy may not appear. For this to be successful, a great general must create a true appointment with the enemy, by encouraging him to arrive on the scene. This is achieved by the careful use of spies who deliver just the right amount of information. Information which divulges false data and encourages the enemy to advance.

67. Follow the rules, and adapt to the enemy until you can fight a decisive battle.

The rules are only meant to be followed while there is uncertainty, however, when the general is very clear on the next steps to be taken, decisive action can be taken, the rules can be discarded and victory can be secured.

68. Present the timidity of a young lady, until the enemy leaves an opening; after move swiftly like a cheetah, and it will be too late for the enemy to defend against you.

CHAPTER 12 - THE ATTACK BY FIRE

1. There are five ways to attack with fire:

    1.   Burn the soldiers in their camp.

Set fire to the enemy's camp and burn them to death.

    2.   Burn the supplies.

Set fire to the enemy's provisions, food and fuel.

    3.   Burn the transport.

Set fire to the enemy's vehicles.

    4.   Burn the weapons and ammunition.

Set fire to the enemy's weapons, ammunition and equipment (including uniform and protective clothing).

    5.   Throw fire at the enemy.

Shoot fire into the enemy's camp by lighting arrows and firing them into enemy territory.

2. To attack we must have the means available.

For a successful attack we have to have the right circumstances in our favour, the right terrain, the resources and above all the right skill developed through training.

3. There are particular times suited for making attacks with fire, and special days for starting infernos.

4. The correct season is when the climate is very dry; the special days are when the moon is in the constellations of the Sieve, the Wall, the Wing or the Cross-bar.

These are the 7th, 14th, 27th, and 28th of the Twenty-eight Stellar Mansions, roughly corresponding to Sagittarius, Pegasus, Crater and Corvus, as these are all days of rising wind.

5. When attacking with fire, one should be prepared for five possible developments:

6. (1) When fire breaks out inside to enemy's camp, respond immediately with an attack from the outside.

7. (2) If there is an outbreak of fire, but the enemy's soldiers do not react, wait patiently and do not attack. The objective of attacking with fire is to send the enemy into utter confusion. If this does not happen, it means that the enemy is ready for us. Be cautious.

8. (3) When the flames reach their height, launch an attack, if possible; if not, stay where you are.

If you see a possible way to attack, do so, but if you see difficulties - do not advance.

9. (4) If it is possible to launch an attack with fire from the outside, do not attempt do to it from within, deliver your attack as soon as you can.

Setting the enemy's camp on fire from within is harder than doing it from the outside. To do so from within requires soldiers infiltrating the camp which is a huge risk. If an attack with fire can be done from a distance, externally, it is preferable.

10. (5) When you start a fire, do so in a way that the wind moves it toward your target. Do not start a fire which is sheltered from the wind.

11. A day breeze lasts a long time, but ends when night falls.

A strong wind does not last longer than a morning, a day breeze lasts longer but ends at night, and a night breeze ends at the break of day.

12. Every army should know of the five developments connected with fire, how to calculate the stars and the correct days for attack.

Not only should a general know how to determine the correct times for attack, but also when the times are favourable how to be prepared for the same attacks incoming from the enemy.

13. Therefore, a general who can use fire as an additional to the attack shows intelligence; and one who can use water as well gains an accession of strength.

14. By using water, an enemy may be intercepted, but cannot be stripped of all his possessions.

Water can be used to divide roads, block paths, and split an army's men in two, however it does not possess the capability of fire which can not only cause death, but can also be used to destroy the enemies supplies.

15. A general wins his battles and succeeds in his attacks without cultivating a spirit of enterprise will meet an unhappy fate; as overall result is waste of time and general inertia.

It is of utmost importance to always maintain a spirit of enterprise, to make use of the opportunities provided, whether that be to attack with fire, or attack with water, and when applied to the day to day life of a person, not only a general, enterprise is what generates consistent results and positive improvements. To merely hold on to the favourable circumstances which have already been granted, and not be productive in seizing others, leads to an ultimate end which will not be a pretty sight. Everything changes, and therefore, enterprise is a shield against misfortune.

16. The enlightened general lays his plans well in advance; and a good general develops his resources.

A great general, controls his men with authority, and they band together due to their faith in him. He rewards them and they remain loyal. If their faith diminishes there will be disorder, and if they go unrewarded – the general's commands will not be accepted.

17. Move only if you see an advantage; do not utilise your soldiers unless something is to be gained; do not fight unless in a desperate position.

18. A general should not utilise his soldiers purely to gratify his own anger; a general should not fight a battle purely out of irritation.

19. Move forward if it is advantageous; if not, stay where you are.

20. With time anger may turn in to happiness; annoyance be replaced with contentedness.

21. A kingdom which has been destroyed can never be restored to its former state.

As the dead cannot be brought back in to life.

22. The enlightened general is careful; a good general is full of caution. This is the way to keep a country at peace and an army intact.

On the flipside: unless you enter the lion's den, you can never take the lion's cubs. A great general will know how to exercise caution, but also knows when it is appropriate to move forward for advantage.

CHAPTER 13 - THE USE OF SPIES

1. Moving a hundred thousand men across great distances entails heavy drain on the people and resources of the State. There will be chaos at home and abroad.

In historic times of war civilian men were forced to join the army, and taken from their homes, leaving the household devoid of the man, for a woman devoid of her husband and for their children, devoid of their father. The households were heavily taxed to support the army.

When an army is in hostile territory it may forage on a captured enemy's supplies and land, but when this is not possible, there is a heavy reliance on transported supplies and that which is taken from the home country.

In summary: any war with a necessity for movement over great distance, is extremely taxing on the people and the state.

2. Adverse armies may oppose for many years, striving for a victory which can decided a single day. This being so, to remain in ignorance of the enemy's condition by use of spies, simply because one does not want to pay for their services, is the height of foolishness.

The use of spies allows one to determine the condition of the enemy and his soldiers and provides one with the information to calculate the appropriate time for attack. Every day that the war continues costs a substantial amount more than the use of spies. If one does not understand this, the cost of immeasurably greater.

3. One who acts without their use is no leader of men, no help to his state, and no master of victory.

Paradoxically the true objective in war is peace. The end objective is to restore harmony and balance between the King, general, army, and civilian population, and also to redistribute proportionately the wealth among them.

4. What enables the wise King and great general to command and conquer, and achieve what is beyond the reach of ordinary men, is foresight.

Foresight: intelligence of the enemy's condition and plans, to know his intentions beforehand.

5. This foresight cannot be extracted from spirits; and it cannot be merely from past experience, or by deductive calculation.

Precise measurements like length, breadth, distance and magnitude, cannot be mathematically determined without knowledge; and likewise, human actions cannot be so calculated.

6. Knowledge of the enemy's condition and plans can only be obtained from other men.

Information in natural science can be obtained with inductive reasoning; the laws of the universe can be verified by mathematical calculation: but the condition and plans of an enemy are only ascertainable through spies and spies alone.

7. Therefore there are five types of spies:

> (1) Local spies
> (2) Inward spies.
> (3) Converted spies.
> (4) Doomed spies.
> (5) Surviving spies.

8. When all five types are at work, no one can discover the secret system. This is called "divine manipulation of the threads." It is the state's most precious faculty.

9. Local spies means employing the services of the inhabitants of a region.

In the enemy's country, win the favour of the inhabitants by treating them kindly and then use them as spies.

10. Inward spies means making use of officials of the enemy.

These can be disgruntled men who have lost rank, or are unhappy about being in a subordinate position. Those which have been punished for acts they have or haven't committed. Those that are fearful that they will be on the losing side. Indecisive men who are always wavering what side to be on.

In all cases these men should be approached secretly and lured with great gifts. By doing so, you can obtain information about the enemy's condition and what plans are being formed against you. You also create disharmony among the enemy and his men.

11. Converted spies means capturing the enemy's spies and using them for our own purposes.

Utilise heavy bribes and promises of freedom, and subsequently have these spies carry back false information and spy on their original employers.

Alternatively, a great general may pretend not to have detected the spy and then lead him to believe false information and carry this back.

12. Doomed spies means performing deliberate actions for purposes of deception, and allowing our own spies to know and carry them to the enemy.

This essentially means, deliberately giving false information to our own spies knowing they will be captured. The enemy will then act on this information and find that the general does something very different.

13. Surviving spies, finally, are those who bring back information from the enemy.

A surviving spy should be a man of superior intellect, yet appear to be a fool in person, and possess a will of iron.

Physically strong and courageous, ready for hard work, able to endure cold and hunger, shame and humiliation.

14. In the whole army – no one is more privileged with intimate relations than spies.

A spy has greater access to information than any other in an army, and may find himself invited in to a general's office. No other is as greatly rewarded, and in no other business should as much secrecy be well-kept.

*All information should be carried from mouth to ear.
Spies are most loyal to those who give them the most.*

They should never be known to any one, or know one another.

Hold their possessions, wife or children as ransom to ensure their loyalty.

Never provide them with information beyond what is absolutely necessary.

15. Spies will not be useful without possessing intuitive discernment.

Successful spies must be able to determine what is true and what is false, and know the difference between honesty and deceit. They require practical intelligence, and an intuitive perception. Before utilising them, we must be sure of their character, experience and skill. However, an undistinguishable face and ability to be underhanded, makes this almost impossible to determine. It takes a man of genius to know.

16. Spies cannot be managed properly without generosity and directness.

When you have gained their favour with great gifts, a general must be straightforward and direct in order to get the best use of out them.

17. Without possessing ingenuity of mind, a general cannot guarantee the truth of their reports.

A general must be perceptive and aware of the possibility of a spy converting and being of service to the enemy.

18. Be careful, but use your spies for every kind of business.

19. If a spy divulges secret information before the agreed time, he and whoever was told must be murdered.

If information has been let out before a general has been able to execute his plans, the spy must be killed as a punishment for the deed, but those who heard are murdered to prevent any further spread of information. However, if the information has already spread, the murder of those who the secret was told to, would not have the desired effect. Yet the general may very well wish to kill anyway as they may have forced the spy to leak information.

20. If the objective is to destroy an army, take a city, or to assassinate an individual, it is always necessary to begin by finding out the names of the attendants, door-keepers and guards of the general in command. Our spies must be appointed to ascertain these.

All of this information can be gained through bribes.

21. The enemy's spies must be discovered, bribed and housed in luxury. They will then become converted spies and available for our use.

22. With information gained from converted spies we can acquire and employ local and inward spies.

The enemy's spies know the local inhabitants and officials which are open to corruption.

23. With this information, we can use a doomed spy to carry false information to the enemy.

A converted spy knows how to best deceive the enemy.

24. With converted spy information, surviving spies can be used on appointed occasions.

25. The main goal of spying using all five varieties is knowledge of the enemy; and this knowledge can only be originated, in the first instance, from a converted spy.

Not only does a converted spy bring knowledge, he makes it possible to make use of all other types of spies with greater advantage.

Therefore, a converted spy must be treated with the utmost importance.

26. The rise of Shang dynasty which was renamed the Yin dynasty was due to I Chih, otherwise known as I Yin, the famous general and statesman. The rise of the Chou dynasty was due to Lu Ya.

Here two famous generals are named as examples to follow. Research famous successful generals and learn from them, their thoughts, and their histories.

27. The enlightened and wise general will use the highest intelligence of the army for purposes of spying and consequently achieve exceptional results.

Just as a boat may carry an army from shore to shore, it quite possibly may sink and be the end of the army. Likewise, the use of spies may be the greatest thing a general can utilise, yet in many cases, spies may actually cause the total destruction of the general's army.

However, spies are the most essential component in war, because without them the general executes random moves.

An general without spies is like a man without eyes or ears.

END

For more adapted classics by James Harris
please visit:

Http://ViewAuthor.at/JamesHarris

Printed in Great Britain
by Amazon

17658516R00068